MW00744661

God's Little Christmas Book

HB
HONOR
BOOKS

Honor Books
Tulsa, Oklahoma

God's Little Christmas Book, mini edition
ISBN 1-56292-761-2
Copyright © 1999 by Honor Books
P.O. Box 55388
Tulsa, Oklahoma 74155

References

Introduction

On that wonderful night in the obscure, tiny town of Bethlehem, God kept His promise and declared His eternal love for us by sending His Son, Jesus—the Christ, the anointed One—as flesh and blood. Emmanuel: God with us!

The angels burst forth from heaven, singing and rejoicing at the long-awaited birth of the King of kings—the Messiah—whose arrival had been foretold by the Jewish prophets. Shepherds bowed in awe, and the Wise Men, who had followed the beautiful, bright star from their homelands, knelt and offered their gifts to the Christ child, the Lamb of God, lying in a hay-filled manger.

Through the beauty of the Scriptures, songs, traditions, and poetry, *God's Little Christmas Book* in this keepsake mini edition celebrates God's gracious gift to the world—our Lord and Savior Jesus Christ!

God sent the angel *Gabriel* to the *Galilean* village of *Nazareth* to a virgin engaged to be married to a man descended from *David*. . . . The angel assured her, "*Mary*, you have nothing to fear. *God* has a surprise for you: You will become pregnant and give birth to a son and call his name *Jesus*. He will be great, be called 'Son of the Highest.'"

Luke 1:26,27,30-32 THE MESSAGE

A Holy, Happy Christmas.

*Our first Christmas gift is
the Gift of gifts, Jesus
Himself, the Son of God.
The tiny babe in the crib has
conquered all hearts. His
birthday has become a day of
joy for the whole world.*

❄

As each one has received a gift,
minister it to one another,
as good stewards of the
manifold grace of God.

⁓ 1 Peter 4:10 NKJV ⁓

The practice of singing Christmas carols appears to be almost as old as the celebration of the day itself. In the first days of the Church, the bishops sang carols on Christmas Day, recalling the songs sung by the angels at the birth of Christ.

❄

Praise him for his majestic glory, the glory of his name.

Psalm 29:1

In Italy, the Presepio or crib is as characteristic of Christmas as the tree in Germany. Every home, even the poorest, has a Presepio of some kind, and the churches have very elaborate ones. The people place humble gifts of nuts and apples in the hands of the life-sized figures.

✼

Whatever measure you use to give—large or small—will be used to measure what is given back to you.

≈ Luke 6:38 ≈

For centuries, the voice of the bell has been heeded with reverence on all occasions and Christmas is no exception. All around the world, the joyous pealing of bells and melodious strains of chimes welcome the birth of the Savior.

At once the angel was joined by a huge
angelic choir singing God's praises:
"Glory to God in the heavenly heights."

❧ Luke 2:13-14 THE MESSAGE ❧

There is no name so sweet on earth, no name so sweet in heaven, the name, before His wondrous birth, to Christ the Savior given.

— George W. Bethune

❄

He is the image of the invisible God, the firstborn over all creation.

Colossians 1:15 NIV

The First Christmas

Joseph went from the Galilean town of Nazareth up to Bethlehem in Judah, David's town, for the census. As a descendant of David, he had to go there. He went with Mary, his fiancée, who was pregnant. While they were there, the time came for her to give birth. She gave birth to a son, her firstborn. She wrapped him in a blanket and laid him in a manger, because there was no room in the hostel.

Luke 2:4-7 THE MESSAGE

A touching and beautiful Christmas custom is observed at early Mass on Christmas morning in some parts of South America. As the Nativity is reenacted, an Indian lullaby is sung to quiet the Christ Child in His cradle of straw. The music of little bells and rattles can be heard as worshippers celebrate the Divine Birth.

The Birth of Christ.   Die heilige Nacht.

*I*t was the day before Christmas, 1818. In the little village of Oberndorf, something had gone wrong with the church organ. Father Joseph Mohr worried that there would be no music for the Midnight Mass. Then he had an inspiration. He would write a new song and have Franz Gruber compose a simple melody suited to guitar and mandolin.

Gruber worked feverishly on the score, leaving time for only a brief rehearsal. In the more than 100 years that have passed since its composition, "Silent Night, Holy Night" has been sung throughout the world.

Silent night, holy night!

All is calm, all is bright

Round yon Virgin, Mother and Child,

Holy Infant so tender and mild!

Sleep in heavenly peace,

Sleep in heavenly peace.

—Joseph Mohr and Franz Gruber

In the Ukraine, singers stroll through the villages carrying a manger and singing folk songs, which tell of the birth of Christ.

✳

The shepherds told everyone what had happened and what the angel had said to them about this child.

Luke 2:17

The earth has grown old
with its burden of care,
But at Christmas it always is young,
The heart of the jewel
burns lustrous and fair,
And its soul full of music
bursts forth on the air,
When the song of the angels is sung.

— *Phillips Brooks*

❄

Wherever your treasure is, there
your heart and thoughts will also be.

⟿ Luke 12:34 ⟿

The First Eyewitnesses

As the angel choir withdrew into heaven, the sheepherders talked it over. "Let's get over to Bethlehem as fast as we can and see for ourselves what God has revealed to us." They left, running, and found Mary and Joseph, and the baby lying in the manger.

Luke 2:15-16 THE MESSAGE

The first Noel the angel did say
Was to certain poor shepherds
in fields as they lay;
In fields where they lay,
keeping their sheep,
On a cold winter's night that was so deep.
Noel, Noel,
Noel, Noel,
Born is the King of Israel.

❄

He will feed his flock like a shepherd;
he will carry the lambs in his arms
and gently lead the ewes with young.

≈ Isaiah 40:11 ≈

In Egypt, Christians burn candles, lamps, and logs in great numbers on Christmas Eve, as symbols of the "Shepherds' Fire."

❄

For You will light my lamp; the LORD my God will enlighten my darkness.

⟪ Psalm 18:28 NKJV ⟫

According to legend, when the shepherds came to Bethlehem, they found the Holy Family suffering from the cold. The youngest shepherd went out and gathered a bundle of ash sticks to kindle a fire, and even though the wood was green, the fire immediately burned brightly.

By the light and warmth of this blaze, the newborn Babe was washed and swaddled. To this day, although the sap of all other woods prevents their kindling, the ash retains its ability to burn even when freshly cut.

Plum Pudding and Mince Pie

Originally called "Christmas pudding" and "Christmas pie," the mixture of spices in these desserts represents the gifts brought to the Infant Christ by the Wise Men.

According to an ancient folk story, the fire that had been built to keep the Christ Child warm as He lay in His manger slowly began to die out. Seeing this, a little robin hopped up to the fire and flapped its wings in an effort to fan the embers back to life.

As it fanned, the breast feathers of the little bird radiated the glow of the fire and turned red. They remain so to this day.

Even the sparrows and swallows are
welcome to come and nest among your
altars and there have their young.

❧ Psalm 84:3 ❧

After Jesus was born in Bethlehem village, Judah territory—this was during Herod's kingship—a band of scholars arrived in Jerusalem from the East. They asked around, "Where can we find and pay homage to the newborn King of the Jews? We observed a star in the eastern sky that signaled his birth. We're on pilgrimage to worship him."

Matthew 2:1-2 THE MESSAGE

*Three Kings came
riding from far away,
Melchoir, and Gaspar,
and Balthasar;
Three Wise-Men out
of the East were they,
And they traveled by night
and they slept by day.
For their guide was a beautiful,
wonderful star.*

— Henry Wadsworth Longfellow

❄

I am . . . the Bright and Morning Star.

Revelation 22:16 NKJV

A JOYFUL CHRISTMAS

What star is this,
with beams so bright,
Which shames the
sun's less radiant light?
It shines to announce
a newborn King—
Glad tidings of our God to bring.

— *Translated from the Latin*
by Rev. J. Chandler
Hymns of the Primitive Church

❄

God is so glorious that even
the moon and stars are less than
nothing as compared to him.

Job 25:5

This old, sobbing world of ours is one year older than it was when the last Christmas carol was chanted. It has had another twelve months of experiments and experiences; of advancement on many lines of human research, scientific discovery, and acquisition. But it has not outgrown Jesus Christ. For Him, it has discovered no substitute. The Star of Bethlehem is the only star that never sets.

— T. L. Cuyler

According to an ancient folktale, when Christ was born, an olive tree, a date palm, and a fir tree stood about the manger. To honor the newborn King, the olive gave its fruit and the palm its dates as an offering, but the fir tree had nothing to give.

Observing this from their lofty perch, a number of stars gently descended from the heavens and rested on the boughs of the fir tree, making it the first Christmas tree.

The stars in the bright sky

Look'd down where He lay,

The little Lord Jesus

Asleep on the hay.

—James R. Murray

❄

For God loved the world so
much that he gave his only Son.

～ John 3:16 ～

In Ireland, candles are placed in the windows on Christmas Eve. They are intended to serve as a guide and an invitation to all who, like Mary and Joseph on the first Christmas Eve, may be wandering about unable to find quarters for the night.

On this special night, poor wanderers and tramps are welcomed everywhere.

With Best
Christmas Wishes.

Rosemary was once considered a Christmas green, along with holly, mistletoe, and ivy. It was admired for its fragrance rather than its color.

According to an ancient folktale, rosemary acquired its fragrance when Mary hung the swaddling clothes worn by the Christ Child on a rosemary bush to dry.

Christmas Wish.

Where the berries glisten.
Berries white and fine.
(None to say or listen)
Kisses sweet be thine.

Herod then arranged a secret meeting with the scholars from the East. Pretending to be as devout as they were, he got them to tell him exactly when the birth-announcement star appeared. Then he told them the prophecy about Bethlehem, and said, "Go find this child. Leave no stone unturned. As soon as you find him, send word and I'll join you at once in your worship."

⟞ Matthew 2:7-9 THE MESSAGE ⟝

$\mathcal{D}$own the narrow street swayed three tall, richly harnessed camels, carrying three strangers in costly raiment. They halted in front of the house of Lemuel and dismounted.

They were Wise Men of the East. . . . They said that a sign in the sky had led them to do homage to a heavenly King whose coming was foretold. . . . So they let down their corded bales and brought out gifts of gold and frankincense and myrrh. Kneeling in the house, they presented their tribute to the child Jesus.

—Henry Van Dyke

The Magi of the East,

in sandals worn,

Knelt reverent, sweeping round,

With long pale beards, their

gifts upon the ground,

The incense, myrrh, and gold.

— *Elizabeth Barrett Browning*

❄

His mercy goes on from
generation to generation,
to all who reverence him.

Luke 1:50

*I*n France, only the children receive gifts. In some parts of the country, a youth is dressed in white and wears a crown set around with many little candles. He is said to represent the Christ child and carries a bell and a basket full of goodies.

Another person carrying a bunch of switches accompanies the youth. At the sight of him, naughty little boys and girls hide. The youth representing the Christ child asks that they be forgiven. Once the children promise to behave better, they are given their gifts and shown the Christmas tree.

The first real Christmas cards appear to have been printed in London in 1846. Almost 1,000 copies were made—that would have been considered a large sale at the time.

It was not until about 1860 that the custom became popular. The tradition has gained strength through the years, and today, Christmas cards are produced by the millions.

Now here is my greeting which
I am writing with my own hand. . . .
May the blessing of our Lord
Jesus Christ be upon you all.

◦◦ 2 Thessalonians 3:17-18 ◦◦

In Spain, children receive their gifts from the Wise Men, especially Balthasar.

The children place their shoes in rows by the doors and windows, where the Wise Men, repeating their pilgrimage each year, will see them and fill them with toys and good things.

A MERRY
CHRISTMAS

AND A HAPPY NEW YEAR.

The gifts of the Magi were symbolic of their three-fold faith: The gold signified that He was King, the incense that He was God, and the myrrh that He was man.

✸

For in Christ there is all of God in a human body. . . . He is the highest Ruler, with authority over every other power.

⟿ Colossians 2:9-10 ⟿

St. Nicholas is vested as a bishop in European countries. Santa was given his change of clothes and became a laughing, red-faced, bewhiskered gentleman here in America.

❄

For the LORD is great and
greatly to be praised.

1 Chronicles 16:25 NKJV

Legend has it that the popular custom of using stockings to hold gifts and goodies on Christmas originated one Christmas Eve when St. Nicholas dropped a purse of money down the chimney as a gift to a poor family. Instead of falling on the hearth, the purse rolled into a stocking on the floor, where it was found the next morning.

Let us stop just saying we love
people; let us really love them,
and show it by our actions.

◆◆◆ 1 John 3:18 ◆◆◆

The Word became flesh and blood, and moved into the neighborhood. We saw the glory with our own eyes, the one-of-a-kind glory, like Father, like Son, generous inside and out, true from start to finish.

Joy is simply love looking at its treasures. A Christian's joy is in loving Christ and loving other people because Christ loves them; it is in doing good to others, and so having a Christmas perpetually.

— T. L. Cuyler

❋

We love Him because
He first loved us.

∽ 1 John 4:19 NKJV ∽

On Christmas Eve in Lithuania, a layer of hay is placed under the tablecloth in memory of the night Jesus was born in Bethlehem, and a wafer, symbolizing the love and harmony of the season, is shared by all present.

Remember His covenant always,
the word which He commanded,
for a thousand generations.

❧ 1 Chronicles 16:15 NKJV ❧

In Norway, before retiring on Christmas Eve, the shoes of all the members of the household are placed in a row as a symbol that everyone will live peacefully together during the year. Instead of wishing others a "Merry Christmas" the next morning, the member of the household who wakes first sings a little hymn.

A personal Jesus accepted means salvation; a personal Jesus obeyed is sanctification; a personal Jesus followed is a life of brotherly kindness and true philanthropy; a personal Jesus reigning in the heart is the fullness of peace and joy and power. The bells of Bethlehem ring one note; the Christmas carols are all calling aloud the same note: "Back to Christ!" "Back to Christ!"

—T. L. Cuyler

Tell me the story of Jesus,

Write on my heart

ev'ry word;

Tell me the story most precious,

Sweetest that ever was heard.

—*Fanny J. Crosby*

❄

Behold, You desire truth in the
inward parts, and in the hidden part
You will make me to know wisdom.

Psalm 51:6 NKJV

CHRISTMAS
THOUGHTS

In Denmark, after returning from church on Christmas Eve, the whole family joins hands and sings carols while marching round the brightly decorated tree.

❄

Sing to the LORD, all the earth;
proclaim the good news of
His salvation from day to day.

∽ 1 Chronicles 16:23 NKJV ∽

A HAPPY NEW YEAR TO YOU

At Christmas, be merry and thank God of all, And feast thy poor neighbours, the great with the small.

— Thomas Tusser

❅

You feed them with blessings from your own table and let them drink from your rivers of delight.

⟿ Psalm 36:8 ⟿

*Selfishness makes
Christmas a burden;
love makes it a delight.*

❄

Do to others what you
would have them do to you!

⟨ Matthew 7:12 NIV ⟩

The only blind person at Christmastime is he who has not Christmas in his heart.

—Helen Keller

We have seen his glory, the glory of the One and Only, who came from the Father, full of grace and truth.

John 1:14 NIV

If you have enjoyed this book, or
if it has impacted your life, we
would like to hear from you.
Please contact us at:

Honor Books
Department E
P.O. Box 55388
Tulsa, Oklahoma 74155
Or by e-mail at: info@honorbooks.com

Additional copies of this book and other
titles in the *God's Little Instruction Book*
series are available from your
local bookstore.